Exit Lines

poems by

Kevin Brown *18 December 2009*

To Monica,

who helped me to be better, through her example
and actions.

Kev

Plain View Press
P. O. 42255
Austin, TX 78704

plainviewpress.net
sb@plainviewpress.net
512-441-2452

Cover art, *This is Not An Exit*, by Danielle Lesperance.
Author photo by Steve Simmerman.

Acknowledgments

Acknowledgment is made to the following publications in which
these poems first appeared: "As If You Could Put the Pieces Together
Again," in *Juked*, February 2008; "Diagramming Won't Help This
Situation," in *REAL: Regarding Arts and Letters*; Summer/Fall 2008;
"The End is Near," in *Paradigm*, Spring 2008; "Exit Lines," in *Words of
Wisdom*, June 2005; "Fortune Telling," in *The Houston Literary Review*,
April 2009; "I Forgot to Ask About the Checkout Time," in *Foliate
Oak*, Fall 2005; "In Search Of," and "Night Sky," in *gtwentytwo*, Spring
2009; "Second Birth," in *gtwentytwo*, Februrary 2009; "Left Standing
at the Altar," in *The Binnacle*, Spring 2007; "The Light of Salvation,"
in *Jeopardy*, 2002-2003; "Love, Over Easy," in *Main Channel Voices*,
December 2008; "Lover's Leap at Rock City," in *The Pacific Review*,
2003; "Moving Day," in *Main Channel Voices*, Fall 2007; "November
13, 1998," in *The TMP Irregular*, Fall 1999; "Playing Dead," in *Timber
Creek Review*, Summer 2005; "Serving Grace," in *3.1.6.: A Journal
of Christian Thinking*, Autumn 2007; "Snow Days," in *The Binnacle*,
Spring 2007; "Summer Shower," in *Nebo*, Spring 2005; "A Vocabulary
of Faith," in *Words of Wisdom*, March 2005; "A Voice Crying," *3.1.6.*: in
A Journal of Christian Thinking, Autumn 2007; "We Are All Savages,"
in *h2so4*, Autumn/Winter 2004.

For all of those who have
helped to shape my soul
through our relationships

"Hold a book of poetry and
you hold a writer's soul."
~Jane Yardborough

"More and more, it has
seemed to me that the idea
of an individual, the idea
that there is someone to be
known, separate from the
relationships, is simply an
error."
~Mary Catherine Bateson

Contents

I Loved To Hear the Stories

And I remember the stories
you used to tell when we
were young and when I
worshipped you. And

I remember the light in
your eyes that fanned the
flame that fed your fervor.
And I remember the sound

of the song of your spirit
that carried your voice like
a choir of angels. And
I remember your generosity

and gentleness and genuineness
of your touch, the way you
held the world in a hug
laced with a love without end.

But most of all, I remember
the stories, and neither the
nothingness you pretend to
preach now, the sanctity

of the self that you slather
onto your speech, nor the idolatry
of idleness you kowtow before,
will ever force me to forget.

Conjugation

My friends assure me that
it is enough to have been.

They do not understand that
to have written is not the same
as wrestling with words,
capturing ideas that will escape
from humanity, if neglected.

They do not comprehend that
to have believed is not the same
as staring down demons
so that, if I do not defeat them,
at least I will know their names.

They do not recognize that
to have loved is not the same
as holding one's hand out into
the void of life because I know
there is someone there to grab it.

The past participle reminds me
that life has passed me by, making
my present far from perfect, a time
in which I do not want to be.

The End Is Near

Perhaps the homeless man
near your house is the
harbinger you have not
yet heard. And perhaps

the prostitute and the pimp
are the prophets whom
you pass and pretend not
to notice. And perhaps

the sounds the schizophrenic
hears come from the
heaven you hope to
obtain. But you do

not know, nor do I, nor do they,
for we have mangled the mystery
of God, we have inoculated

ourselves from the infectious wonder
in our world, and we have murdered
every messiah sent to save us.

Everyone Thinks They're Just Fairy Tales

And no matter how many
skies have fallen, the Chicken
Littles must find their way
around the debris and
destruction of their lives,
avoiding the Foxy Woxies
of the world who seek
only to silence them~
swallow them, if need
be~and find their way to
warn the king, no matter
how many Henny Pennies
think they've lost their minds.

Harbinger

Seeing a well of living water
where others only saw desert,
the Baptist found a savior instead

of a no-name from Nazareth. The
divine has no need of a prophet, if
God be truly there, but we mere

mortals require a John to herald our
journeys. Cursed to wander the
wilderness without one, we must

plumb our depths to find the waves of
wonder waiting to break forth, if only
we could tap them with our divining rod.

A Voice Crying

Our well-fed, store-bought prophets
preach to our Ahabs and Jezebels,
providing comfort to the kingdom,
assuring them that all is well

in the world. And our Elijahs and
Isaiahs are consigned to the desert
where they wander and wonder
about our land that suffers and hurts,

yet will not listen. Those who have ears to
hear have turned up the volume of the TV,
claiming to want to know the state of affairs,
but it is only the glow they wish to see.

Fortune Telling

Completely unlike the
lilies of the field,
betraying the birds
of the air, we seek
to find our future
in the same way
that we have

predicted our past.
We seek signs anywhere~
astrology or 8-balls,
therapists or thespians,
stock markets or our
mothers, tea leaves
or low-interest loans~in

an attempt to tell
tomorrow what it
may or may not hold
in store for us. And
while we arm wrestle
with our destiny, today
has us pinned to the mat.

The Church Of Divine Reality, Inc.

There are laws, you know, legal
liabilities that must be
considered. If Jesus shows up
in a vision, and somebody

veers off the interstate into a
telephone pole, who do you
think they're going to sue?
It's not going to be Jesus, I

can assure you. Or take the
case from a few years ago:
a man rids himself of all
his worldly possessions (well,

except for a camel's hair coat)
and goes all paparazzi on
people, getting in their faces
and screaming about repentance.

Lost his head, he did. And
who did the family go after?
It wasn't the Spirit, as if he or
she or whatever has any type

of representation; he or, you
know, barely has any kind
of manifestation these days.
You see, someone around here

has to store up treasures
and make sure they're protected
from every bit of rust, moth, or
ne'er-do-well who has the Virgin

Mother show up on a burrito.
Someone has to take responsibility
for God, after all; it's not like
we want him running wild.

The Light Of Salvation

We speak of *the* sun,
as if the other stars–
Alpha Centari, Vega,

Beta Orionis, and
Canopus–are not suns
themselves, energy sources for

scores of planets, larger,
smaller, warmer, colder,
different than ours,

but our perspective
blinds us, as if we have
spent too much time

staring at *our* sun.
And, thus, we should not
wonder that we speak

of *the* God we worship,
creating shibboleths of
salvation–meditations and

mantras; prayers and
penance; creeds and
confessions; enlightenment

and evangelism–to ensure
the truth is spread
to those who need it most,

while *our* God
and *their* God
weeps.

The Waves and Whales and Ways Of God

Which did Jonah fear worse:
being tossed into the tempest
or swallowed by a whale?

Is death by drowning the best
alternative, or would one rather
smother in blubber? Either way,
it would be God's wrath
raining down upon him, as
he was to relate to the Ninevites,
which causes one to wonder why

he had no understanding of their
repentance--they are saved in
the same manner he is, but they
needed less dramatic means of
convincing. But, of course, to
Jonah's way of viewing the world,
as in ours, the Ninevites deserved
it, not him and not us.

The Saint Of Lost Things

I light a candle for the baseball
signed by Carl Yastrzemski and
the class ring with an imitation

birthstone, ruby in my case,
in the center. On Sundays, I
say a prayer for the image of

my best friend from middle
school who somehow neglected
to have his picture taken for

the yearbook and for my pet turtle
Tom whom I forgot to feed for
three weeks one December. And

on your feast day, I pray for one
more yesterday when everything
still held true and I did not fear

the tomorrows, which wait for me
like a second-rate bill collector
who would rather break my knee
than see me pay off my debts.

Begging For Blessings

When my knees nag me like
my mother used to when
my memory ignored her
repeated reminders to clean
my room, I wheel and deal

with the deity for another
week of workouts. And
when traffic troubles delay
me from my departure from
my mundane Monday-through-

Friday existence of work, I
cajole and beg my big friend
to clear out at least one lane to let
me go free. But when a woman
of forty hears her doctor mutter

"malignant," or when a father
faces the cold visage of his
firstborn, or when innocent
civilians watch the guilty
politician wagering on war in

his country, they face God with
their fists, stare down the divine,
and dare him to do one more
thing, bring one more plague,
while I wheedle and whine.

Memory Lapse

In foxholes or falling
planes, in dark nights

or even dark days,
and maybe when we

want to win the lottery,
we turn, but not while

we're skimming the
surface of life. On

the days between horror
and hallelujah, the days

between suffering and
salvation, we forget the

name that has become
nothing more than a

plea for help when
all seems hopeless.

Entertaining Angels

Perhaps they would like to play
charades, acting out the scenes
of Gabriel and Michael's
greatest moments, or maybe
they would simply like to watch
a DVD. I'm sure they don't
often have the opportunity to
rest and eat microwaved popcorn,
but then, what kind of movies do
they like? I can't see them enjoying
action or horror, certainly not
anything involving the occult, but
maybe they would like a good
comedy. Then again, perhaps they
like Bergman; that seems like
something they would enjoy.

But now they're getting up, saying
that they really must be going and
that I should take care of myself. I
tell them that I haven't even had time
to serve the hors d'oeuvres, a new
recipe from this month's *Southern
Living*, but they assure me they'll be
back another time, and, next time,
I'll be ready. I'll even have dessert.

Not For All Practical Purposes

Perhaps you think that truth is nothing
more than a pin
we use to burst a blister or
salvage a splinter—
small, sharp pains that are needed, necessary
for ultimate healing. Or

perhaps you think that truth is nothing
more than an antacid or aspirin
we take before bedtime to
remove the slight discomfort in our diaphragm or
the hint of a headache from too much television. But

perhaps the truth is kept
hidden in an obscure corner
of the museum,
behind the stuffed parrots and
pandas, in a glass marked "In Case of
Emergency," and, like a fireman's axe,
it caves in our chests,
rips open our ribs,
and exposes our hungry hearts

to those who have ventured past
the Van Goghs and Monets.

Hermits

Though I started my journey
naked, Fate gave me a coat,
the cut and color of which
have never been in fashion,

either in this world or the
next. He must get them at
a discount, buy them in bulk
or something, as I see others

shuffling through life clad as
I am, though they do not deign
to notice me, as the world ignores
them. We move through this

life, then, like phantoms in the
mist, clutching our coats closer
to prevent the creeping cold and
rain from reaching our souls.

After Effects

Jesus had it easy. After he
arose, he appeared here and
there for forty days before he

arose one last time, his dramatic
departure leaving the disciples
staring into the sky. Lazarus

had to come back to the life he
left, sharing a house with two
sisters, planting grapes behind

the house they had owned since
their parents passed away, unable
to return. But how could Mary

and Martha, or any woman, compare
to the angels he had seen during his
four-day hiatus from drawing breath?

How can anyone's conversation
surpass the words the saints shared
with him? And once you have

wrestled with the angel of death,
the only enemy left to fight is
the tedium of the passing of time.

I Forgot To Ask About the Checkout Time

And it was at that point, in the
midst of my tirade, that
He reminded me that life is
like a cheap motel:

you get the basic necessities, if
you're lucky, some of which may
not work and none of which
will be clean; you'll share
the space with creatures
you would prefer
not to have any contact with;
and your wake-up call
will come
when you least expect it.

And anything else you want,
you'll have to pay dearly for.

Soul Searching

Some people look for happiness
as if it were a button that
had fallen off the dresser,
straining and stretching their

arm through the lint and
dust bunnies that have
mated and multiplied,
waiting for that familiar

sheen of plastic to find
its way under their fingertips,
while, all the while, happiness
is waiting for them in

the kitchen with a cup of
hot chocolate and a rag
to help them clean the dirt
from the knees of their pants.

Think Again

What you thought was
a voice in the wilderness
was nothing more than a

passing car stereo pounding
its message to the unimpressed
masses. And what you

thought was camel hair was
faux fur, as inoffensive to
PETA as most sound bites

are to voters. And what you
thought was light from a bush
that did not burn up was the glow

of a campfire used by your
neighbor as a screen saver.
And what you thought was

the truth had been spun and
spun again, as if it were a
wheel within a wheel.

The Last Sunset

And when the stars
fall freely
from the heavens

like the fireflies that die
in your well-kept backyard

and when the moon and sun
slowly sink
into the earth

as if they were nothing
more than butter between
the pancakes at the local
Kiwanis annual breakfast,

who do you think you will
run to, if not
those neighbors whose names
you do not know,

and

who do you think will
weep with you, if not the

brothers and sisters in your city
whom you pass every day,
not even deigning to
delay your step and
share a word or two?

Yes, they will be the ones
who will
hold you to their hearts,

and you shall see the
time you have wasted when
you should have been

sitting on their front porch
sharing pictures of your past,
telling stores that stoked
the fires and your passions,

or

simply watching the sun set
slowly, sure it will rise
again tomorrow.

Moot Point

Another night falls, and I
kneel to petition for the
dented and the destroyed,
the haughty and the humble,

though the gesture seems a
relic, somehow similar to
sacrificing virgins to
appease a volcano.

Am I merely singing a
soliloquy while the
stars and the ceiling
idly watch?

The host of heaven has
gone on vacation for a
season, while neighbors
weaken and friends deteriorate.

Can I not even leave a
message for the messiah,
or is the call waiting
out of order?

Those who do heal today
die tomorrow, so why
bother with my posturing, my
pontificating, my piety?

Another night falls, and I
take two minutes in the
hope that I'll feel
better in the morning.

Seeing the Light

We think that it will be
like a candle we only
light when the power

ceases to pulse into our
homes, but the truth is
not some tiki-torch we

use to illuminate our
backyard gatherings or
holiday picnics, nor is

it a night light that we
use as a consolation when
our dreams remind us of

realities we wish to
ignore. Instead, its flash
sears saints as easily as

it does devils; its
radiance rips apart the
lives of the lovely and

the losers alike. We
would be better served
if, instead of hording

flashlight batteries,
we spent our seasons
staring at the sun.

Serving Grace

And so we have become
like troublesome customers,
demanding our steak be medium

well and sending it back time
and time again because
anyone can see that *that*

is clearly *not* medium well,
as if God is some sort of
short-order cook taking

orders from the waiters in
their vestments who meander
around mumbling about their

tips, reluctantly serving those
few who still seek their
assistance, and we forget

that we do not deserve the
steak we have, forget
that there are those who

have never seen a steak, and
forget the feeling of its juice
tracing a path down our

chin like the trail of tears we
shed long ago when we first
understood what steak truly was.

Angels Unaware

Why not believe that a small
object you bend over to
retrieve~a rusty key, a lost

scrap of paper with a scribbled
address, or a coin from a
foreign country~contains a

mystery? Or that a beggar could
be a deity? Occasionally, the
universe simply responds, *Yes.*

And sometimes we say,
"Yes," before anyone has
asked the question.

The International Forgiveness Institute

I arrive worried and late after
running errands that I believed
would not wait for another day.

I assume the line will be lengthy,
but I am in the door and almost to
the counter in minutes. I have heard

that there are loopholes, but I want
to leave no doubt as to the
blankness of the slate. The woman

who greets me is beyond cheerful,
positively giddy with the help she
is able to provide, and she assures

me that she will stay with me until
the process is complete. When I ask
her how painful that process will be,

she simply smiles and produces a pile
of paper. Every question she asks is
the same: Why? Why? Why? *Why?*

I have a feeling that I will be answering
her questions for the rest of my life.

Garbage Day

We flippantly discuss the
death of our gods as if
they were unwanted

wedding presents waiting
in the attic for a friend's
nuptials and the opportunity

to pawn them off on someone
else. We take our two-
bit Buddhas and our

chintzy Christs, our
mangled Muhammads and
cracked Krishnas to the

trash dump of our souls.
But behind the curtain
that separates us from our

minds and hearts, the divine
conflict rages, rages against
the dying of their lives.

In Search Of

We meditate in caves,
catacombs, and churches,
seeking our burning bush

to light the way to sainthood,
praying to be tested,
tempted, and even tortured,

often creating our own tribulations
when others won't cooperate.
We wander through our WASPish

wilderness, bemoaning the cup
of suburbia we are forced to
drink, while we long for a true

Gethsemane to bring our bloody
sweat to the surface.
But the meaning of our lives

is too ordinary for a Biblical
saga: we fold the laundry,
mop the floor, and rake the

leaves fall after fall after
fall like Zen monks sweeping
the porch of the monastery.

Assuming that the mountain
top is where truth is revealed,
we ignore the mundane valley of the

shadow of death we walk to
work and home and church
while dreaming of martyrdom.

Getting through the fiery
furnace is easy, but what
good is a religion that won't
help you do the dishes?

A Second Chance, Of Sorts

Bill Buckner has always allowed
that grounder to roll, like eternity,
through his legs; Roy Riegels
has always run the wrong way,

remembered for the wrong
reason; Andres Escobar has always
snuck the ball by his own
goaltender, giving the United

States an unearned victory, and
he will now always be dead,
despite reports that Jesus, Elvis, and
others have survived that threshold.

The almighty They repeatedly
reminds us that there are no do-
overs in the real world, and the
ones we use in childhood are

fictitious as well, at least when
examined rationally. But They
have forgotten forgiveness, which,
it is true, cannot erase the wrongs

from our slates, but sometimes, just
sometimes, it can wash away enough
of the errors to allow us to write
again, to make new marks, to do better.

Alternative History

If Hitler would have become an artist,

and

Einstein had worked as a watchmaker,

would we not have found ways to

pound enemies into submission
with paintings

and

to wage war
by winding our watches,

always making sure the
trains arrived on time?

We Are All Savages

not because of our
crusades for vengeance
or justice

not because of the hopes
we have killed with a
word or glance

not because of our
murderous thoughts of
former lovers or friends

not even because we
deny dignity to the
destitute or dominant

but because
we have our reasons
for doing so

Snow Days

We sat by the radio
frantically changing

channels, searching
not for music, but

the news for once.
These days turned

the neighborhood
ne'er-do-well into

a believer in a God
who could flood the

Earth, not with water,
but with snow that

would keep us out of
school until Graduation

Day. And on the good
days, their God delivered

a taste of that miracle and
provided for our salvation

from another early morning,
another night of homework,

and one more day was
all the heaven we could take.

Undergraduate Poetry

True, they mangle metaphors and
do not comprehend synecdoche or
metonymy (though their ears still
buzz with a high school definition of
onomatopoeia, and alliteration is
somehow still stuck somewhere),
and, while their poems have
more Is than Argus, they do not
truly understand what Donne
did with conceit.

But, if their attempts at poesy
stumble and stagger and
stutter, perhaps it is
because they, like Dr.
Frankenstein, are trying to
cobble together new life
out of the hundreds
and thousands of years of
dead verse we attempt to resurrect
before their very eyes
three days a week.

And, on those days when we look
beyond our blind spots of poetic
prejudice and loosen the stitches
to peel back the skin they have laid
overtop of their feelings, we see
that their rime has more passion
than our cold couplets and more
truth than the rhythms of our hearts can

hear, so, unlike us, who have long since
grown out of such a notion, they still
believe that poetry can
change the world.

And so it does.

For them.

Habits of the Heart

Perhaps John liked locusts
and wild honey, his
personal epicureanism that
we happen to label as
abnormal, much in the same
way that we look askance

at cultures who crave
dog or snails or grasshoppers.
And perhaps he felt
coddled by the camel's hair
that kept him warm in
the cold nights of the

desert, cuddling in a
cave with his coat, as
comfortable as a king
wrapped in silk.
Or perhaps that's what
we tell ourselves to blunt

the preaching of the
prophets and the sacrifice
that will soon be sent our
way if we ignore the mantle
no longer, or perhaps we'll
find our salvation there, too.

A Vocabulary Of Faith

And as the woman
walked away from
the sidewalk evangelist

who, together with the
singing sisters, had
sought to save her

soul, she covered
herself more fully with
her coat and replied,

"This is my salvation."
And she took the
coins that she had

collected and traded
them for a cup of
coffee, which the

waitress brought,
along with her disdain,
though a piece of pie

somehow appeared as
well, and said to her,
"Don't forget to say

grace, honey," to which
she wearily smiled and
said, "This is my grace."

And as she slid into sleep
that night in a bed made
of borrowed belongings,

clothes cast away long
ago, located underneath
the underworld that

others thought they
knew, her mouth
quietly muttered, "Amen."

Soteriology

Somewhere, somehow we
were duped into trading in
our gods for mere mortals,
men and women who

resemble our reflections
in an eternal mirror.
They no longer walk
on water, throw thunder-

bolts, or help the hope-
less, so neither do we.
But I have seen salvation
through the eyes of a

child, a little child who
shall lead us back to
our great gods, back to
our heavens and our hells,

back to our hearts where
salvation has been waiting
patiently for our arrival.

Day One

While we would all like
to believe in those days
when redemption rains over
us like the storm that breaks
the summer heat, there are
often days when the pain
from our acts cannot be kissed
away by our mothers and will
require stitches, leaving a scar.

There are days when we cry
out for heaven's healing, and
God is as silent as the idols
we have put in his place. And
only on those days when faith,
hope, and love have passed
us by like the priests who
preceded the good Samaritan,
have our lives begun.

Epiphany

Yes, I know that I dreamt
that day, and I know that
when I awoke, I held in my

hand the flower I found
in my dream. And it was
on that day that the clear

edges of life bled and
blurred. And it was on
that day that I sensed the

spirit moving across the void.
And it was on that day and only
on that day that I began to believe.

Perfection

The middle-school boy with the
stutter wishes he could be the
amputee who receives too much
pity and sympathy, while the accountant's
desk dreams of being a code-
cracking computer for the CIA.

The sedentary Siamese wakes
from a nap and glances out
the window to envy a hyacinth
bush, and a woman in her second
of twenty-five years dreams of the
marriage that might have been, while
her sister looks at her husband,
then at the bottle of pills at her bedside.

Ordinary Time

Our pain circles us like a
vulture in the desert, and
we analyze, theorize,
and hypothesize it,

wanting to create tragedy
where there is merely suffering.

We seek to carve
ourselves in the image
of Oedipus, Lear, and Hamlet,
seeking to provide

meaning to our lives,
imagining ourselves actors in a

larger-than-life production.
Content to Walter Mitty
our way through life, we
imagine soap operas and

melodramas to create excitement.
But the truth is found in

the front porch stories
told in the dark,
slices-of-life, not drama.
Though the obituaries

carry the highlights, those
who knew us will remember

the freckles on our chin,
the scars that never
healed, and the way we
slurped our soup.

Your Flight May Be Delayed

While, on our best days, most
of us believe we are seasoned
travelers of life,
whisking our way through
unknown airports with

the appropriately-sized carry-
ons as we arrive at
the proper gate as
they announce that boarding
is now beginning. Unfortunately,

the truth is that we lose
our luggage at the wrong
carousel and miss the
connections that can

carry us to our correct
conclusions. We fear
that the others, the
well-traveled, are
watching us, so we avoid

asking the airline agents for
guidance and meander
through the corridors, always
wheeling our suitcase

behind us as it squeaks like
a baby boy left
behind by his parents.

Second Birth

I wonder how Lazarus
appeared to those who did
not know he had

died. Jesus still had his
scars on his second, albeit
brief, visit. Lazarus had been

sick, so we can assume the
death was internally
caused~cancer, heart

attack, tuberculosis,
or some mid-Eastern
disease long since

forgotten. Did the people
speaking to him politely
look away if he coughed up

blood? Or was he shunned
because of his unorthodox re-
birth, like Frankenstein's

monster? Even if they could not
tell, he had to be different
inside. His lungs, liver,

intestines, heart~whatever
it was that stopped
working for some

reason~had been healed. But
maybe he could feel the
difference in the way he

breathed when the wind turned
icy or in the way his heart
beat softer, even when making

love, or in the foods he could
no longer digest. Do the people
who see me not notice,

either, or are they more
civilized than the village Shelley
crafted? Can they not hear the

catch in my voice, which I
hear as an eight-
track player changing

programs? What about my
feet, formerly clay, now solidified
into lead? Perhaps, like Poe's

madman, only I hear my
heartbeat and know
about the death

in my soul, which is
only now being
resurrected.

Heresy

The message, coming
from you, shakes me,
then breaks me, settling

like a ruined heaven in
my heart. If love was
our religion, then I am a

defrocked priest now that
you have exchanged our dogma
of devotion for the scientific

fact of finality. Despite
today's being Sunday, no
one will rise again after this.

Cupid's Pockets Aren't That Deep

It's not about black-clad
women refusing to smile
on a red-letter day protesting
that it's not about

a middle-aged man treating
his wife to dinner at the
restaurant they frequent
every other weekend while
he mistakenly thinks it's about

young lovers using massage
oil and rose petals
to have tantric sex while
they try not to remember
that they think it's about

their single friends, alone
with the VCR, Haagen-Dazs,
and resentment, though
the truth is that it's about

the guilt that comes from
not loving enough the other
days of the year, so
we allow ourselves to be

conned into purchasing love
like a divorced dad in
Daytona who buys his children
for a day a month.

Those with the empty houses have
hope that they'll be filled
one day, but the empty words on

the cards, the empty feelings of
stomachs stuffed with too
much candy, and the empty hearts

pretending to love because they're
scared to be alone can only be
redeemed by a miracle.

Left Standing At the Altar

I'm the chump you cheer
against in movies, the one
the hero has to save his

true love from marrying.
You judge me as evil or
clueless or greedy, a

caricature of what a
groom should be, but
what do you know of

my life outside my five
minutes of screen time?
Maybe I'm marrying for

money because of the
poverty I witnessed as
a child, an action that

would earn a Victorian
woman praise (though
perhaps not in a Jane

Austen movie) condemns
a postmodern American man.
Perhaps I'm merely lonely

and willing to wed a woman
coming out of any relationship,
unashamed to be accepted as

second best, merely to find
a bride. You would do the
same after the years of

loneliness I've felt: lack of
affection from parents and
being an outcast at school

because I was never taught
the social skills necessary to
fit in. So I worked hard

and became a doctor or a
lawyer or whatever high-
income job I have in this

movie, and you even
fault me for that, as if my
achievement reminds you

of what you did not do
with your life. Perhaps
that's why you champion

my challenger, the underdog
who never even finished
high school. You'd like to

believe that you can overcome
your obstacles and walk away
with the beautiful woman, too.

But let me assure you that
your life will resemble mine
more than you'd like. One

day you'll be the jilted John
while the hero in someone
else's story whisks away the

woman you really did care
about. And then the credits
will roll in his story, but

your pain continues long past
the last box of popcorn and
the exit of the cleaning crew.

The Dictionary Of Failed Relationships

I looked up all of the words
you used to describe me:
discontented, self-centered,
dispassionate, and solipsistic,
a new word for me, one
that rolls around in my
mouth like your kiss, a
combination of soft and
hard that you would share only
when you wanted something.

But you abridged your original
definition of me, forgot the words
you once used: generous,
funny, and intelligent, to
name a few; instead you
changed the connotation of
our relationship and left
us with nothing but a tattered
book that could never define
the complexity of our love.

Diagramming Won't Help This Situation

Grammatical rules have always baffled
me, leaving me wondering whether my
life is transitive or intransitive, if I am the
subject or object of my life, and no one
has been able to provide words to describe
my actions, even if they do end in -ly.

But now the problem seems to be with
pronouns: *I* am unwilling to be *him*,
and *you* are unable to be *her*, so *we*
will never be *them*~the ones talking
about what they need from the grocery

store because the Rogers are coming for
dinner tonight; the couple saving for a
vacation, perhaps a cruise to Alaska or a
museum tour of Europe; the two who meet
with a financial advisor to plan their children's

college fund while still managing to set enough
aside for their retirement~and so we will
continue to be nothing more than sentence
fragments, perfectly fine for effect,
but forever looking for the missing
part of speech we can never seem to find.

Bury the Lead

Your sentences, as short as
your tone, leave no doubt
as to the *who*, and, though

I have tried to remind you of
a different time and place,
you assure me that, in today's

news cycle, the *when* and
where are like the ticker
at the bottom of a broadcast,

ever-present and always
present tense. The *what*
has been announced in a

headline with a font that
should be reserved for a
second coming, a story of

unity or a celebration of a
reconciliation, or even perhaps a
mistake on the scale of

DEWEY DEFEATS TRUMAN

Unfortunately, your story spent
so much time on these four
double-yous, I am left

to wonder about the *why* and
ponder *how* I can live
with the broken news.

Exit Lines

I was always out of character,
it seems. While I thought I
could run to you, I stumbled
over missed cues, unspoken

lines, and a background that
never fit our daily drama. At
least actors can count on a
curtain call when the curtain

falls, but I must skulk away to
the shadows as the audience
exits as silently as you did
when you left last night.

No Exit, Stage Left Or Right

And while I once walked
the boards with confidence,
daring any to dialogue

with me, my foils foiled
me by clearing the set,
leaving me to my somber

soliloquies and monotonous
monologues. And while
the rest of the universe

seems well-rehearsed, I am
no longer well-versed—some
might even call me cursed;

thus, I wander down
stage knowing that I have
been upstaged by those off

stage, while the audience
gazes and gapes at the
comedy I have turned to

tragedy and then to travesty.
And while they exit to the rear
of the theater, I stand on a

darkling stage with nothing
but a crumpled playbill and
bad reviews to show for my life.

Equal To Zero

Was I nothing more than
a calculus conundrum to
be solved,

the variables
of my life matching her
goals,

as she tried to
balance our equation?
My x

equaling a law
degree that would cause
her y

to be a new BMW and
lunch at the club? While
she tried

desperately to find
a common denominator, all I
could do

was assure her
that I had never understood
fractions.

Eco-Friendly

Fine.
I shouldn't have
said it, but the
language leapt from my
mouth like a
sailor abandoning ship,

like an acrobat working
without a net, but my
two and a half somersault
with a twist left me

lying flat on my face
at the bottom
of the
big
top.

It was nothing, a
throwaway line, but my
throwaway lines tend to

get recycled, made into
containers that are unable
to hold their original meaning,

the plastic melting under the
heat of her cross-examination,
quickly dissolving into melodrama
(the wringing of hands, what to do,
what to do, what to do).

Better off to take out the
trash, fill up the
landfills of my life with the
rubbish of past relationships,

but all my lovers end up
being environmentalists
of the heart.

Practicing Sexual Immorality

It began with two beagles in the
backyard. Not fighting, of course,
but one still wanting to be alone,
telling the other that they should
leave, they'd caused enough
trouble for one day. And then
there were the movies, the
magazines, and the music:
pop-culture porn, suburban
smut, a white-bread wonderland,
but if abracadabra was the magic
word, I had no idea what it
opened. As I got older and
got a discount card,
I was able to buy books with
techniques and exercises to
improve, as if the big O
is all my life is missing.

Nothing Left To Say

When you walked out the door
for the last time, it did not

feel like I had lost a limb,
feeling phantom pain for what

was once there, much as we
flip light switches in our houses,

even though we know
there's no power.

When I could not call you to
share the news we had been

waiting to hear, it did not
feel like I could not think

of the word for an
object, that it was just

outside my memory,
waiting to be let in.

No, when we said goodbye
and agreed to end it all, it did

not feel like this or that
because it is not a metaphor or

simile; it is the absence of
poetry when two lives cease

to be one, and the words,

unlike the love, simply stop.

Editorial Cartoon

While turning page after page
of some magazine,
The New Yorker or *Harper's*, perhaps,
I can't recall, I see the image

I've seen before in cartoon strips,
sitcoms (the arbiters of truth) or
read in novels, short stories,
even poems:

A married couple standing at the
door, one of them, usually the
woman, though certainly not always,
holding two suitcases, never one or

three, always one for each hand as he
or she prepares to exit, not leaving
on vacation or a business trip, but a
last goodbye, the final exit of love.

But that is not it.
That is not it at all.

There are no pictures of lying in bed
next to one you once loved, trying to
sleep, to forget what is real,

no drawings of the two of you visiting
relatives, smiling like newlyweds,
though everyone there knows the truth,

no sketches of eating out, asking
about the others' work just so you
won't have to eat out alone,

and no cartoons of affairs, abuse,
verbal or physical, children used
as pawns in the petty power struggle,

no poems of arguments between
lawyers, strangers made privy to our
innermost secrets in order to get the TV.

But that is it.
Though that is not all.

Leftovers

She sits at the kitchen table
wondering where she can
scrounge supper while

she pays a pile of bills,
the memory of the man
who most recently left.

She can hear *Wheel of
Fortune* coming from
the next room where her

children, the only other
remains of her relationships,
hopefully watch the television.

Method Acting

I have tried to do Dean and be
Brando (Kowalski, not Malloy,
as I can still be a contender),
believing that my mumblings
would convey true emotion
better than following some
script of what I am supposed to
say. While others were wowed
by my performance, the only
critic who matters was left
cold, so I have gone back
on book, attempting to learn
the lines that will convey the
character of my heart. In the
meantime, I wait for my agent
to call with news that the
studio would like a sequel.

Not What It Seems

I am not writing you a love
poem. You do not wish to
hear the saccharine similes I
have to share; after all, your
eyes and lips are not like
anything; they are simply
where I wish to look and
what I want to kiss. So,

I am not writing you a love
poem. The meaningless rhymes
of love make it seem as if
it comes from above or fits
like a glove, but it, like nothing
else, is of this earth, as it
chafes our hearts and hands,
rubbing them both raw. Thus,

I am not writing you a love
poem. My metaphors mean
nothing to you, as our love is
not a red, red rose or a many-
splendored thing; instead it is a
sledgehammer to the knees, its
single-mindedness focusing us on
the only goal we ever knew. As such,

I am not writing you a love
poem. When faced with the
blank page, I will fold it into a
butterfly and give that to you
instead, so that you will understand
the fragility of life and love in
a way that my words have
never seemed able to express.

Moving Day

On the day that I helped you
carry your futon down the five
flights of stairs we had carried
it up four years before, I realized
I was doomed to be an eternal
moving man, only now I would
carry your departure with me as
if it were a worn-out, soiled sofa
bed, which, if it were not heavy
enough because of the extra
weight within the crusty cushions,
isn't even comfortable for a decent
night's sleep due to the metal bar of
remorse that keeps me from forgetting
you whenever I close my eyes.

Love, Over-Easy

The biscuits lie
scattered and tattered,
covered with
tepid gravy,
not quite half-eaten

while the dirty
dishes sit soaking
in the sink and the
dish towel hangs
askew on its rod.

The pepper is over-
turned on the table, where
she left it when he
spoke, and the door remains
open, where she exited.

Not For Nostalgia's Sake

And now, after only a few
days, you are already an
anecdote, a story I tell
to continue a conversation
about food, music, or just

women. And your picture
is buried in my box of
memories, under high school
yearbooks and a baseball
card collection that doesn't
even have sentimental value

these days. Yet I know that,
like a shy relative who only
visits on special occasions,
you will reappear when I'm

distracted, on hold with
customer service perhaps, and
I will see you clearly, but
only to have to watch you
walk out again and again.

Playing In the Sand

I know your time is limited,
my time, everybody's time,
but especially our time,

so I memorize every moment:
the last song we hear together;
our last supper, clichéd as that
may be; even our fight, just

last night. I vow to sketch your
portrait on my heart and to etch
our remaining time on my mind

as Doré did for Dante's descent.
Yet those sketches and etchings
are sandcastle monuments I build
to you now that the tide is out,

and I already hear the waves
of time crashing behind me.

Modern Relationships

Repetition, which I have
wielded like a caveman's
club whenever his woman
wanted to roam, has lost

its effectiveness. Though
my voice leaves scratches
on the coffee table and its
imprint in the cushions of

the couch as I say again and
again what she wants to hear,
she easily sidesteps my
words on her way out the door.

Subject-Verb-Object

Instead of using "I love
you" to get
women into bed or
men into marriage (or
vice versa in our gender-
bending days),

we should put it high
on a shelf
over the refrigerator,
the one we always
forget about,

behind glass that we must
shatter with our elbows and
our illusions,

saving it only for times of
emergency, such as the death
of a child
or the birth
of one, as well. So that when
we say it truly, our lips

end in a pucker, sending
our words
out into the world
with a kiss, expecting
nothing less in return.

Fall

The cold in the air today
did not remind me of
the weekend we spent in
the mountains, waiting
for the trees to explode
with color, while we
pretended that the fire
from our first
days had not faded.

Nor did it remind me of
the midnight air on the
day you told me you were
leaving, your words crackling
in the cold like the bacon
you made me for breakfast
the first morning after
we admitted our love.

No, the changing temperature
took me back to autumn
afternoons when I believed that
I was Bradshaw, driving my
team down the field for the
win or that I could growl
like Mean Joe Greene in a
goal-line stand, catching
the back in the air and
driving him to the ground.

The cold in the air today took me
back to the days when the worst
pain I felt was the incomplete
pass that went in and out of
my hands in the end

zone or a linebacker laid me
out, but, on those days, I could still
redeem myself by soaring like a
Swann for the touchdown that
would send us home as heroes.

As If You Could Put the Pieces Together Again

Broken hearts have become clichés,
especially in poetry, leading to

bad verse, maudlin movies, and
stories students turn in for a first-

year creative writing course. But
in the long term, it's not the

hearts that break that much
matter. Instead, it's the lawn

mower belt that cracks in two when
you're halfway through your yard on

a Saturday afternoon, but not just
any Saturday afternoon, as you later

relate to your relatives, but the
afternoon before the family

reunion you were supposed to
host that night. Or it's

the toilet that overflows on
an ordinary Tuesday evening

as you prepare for bed, keeping
you up hours past your planned

bedtime the night before the
pivotal presentation to your boss.

Unlike Humpty Dumpty, hearts can
and are put back together again and

again, but your sore knee will haunt
you for the rest of your days.

Summer Shower

I used to wait for
you~in the sun,
not the shade, with
sweat trailing down

my cheek, like a tear.
I yearned for your
arrival, wishing that
I could believe you

into being beside me,
much like the women
who prayed for my
grandfather, who died

anyway. And now I
sit in the sun, not the
shade, and wait for
her, whoever she may

be, and the sweat
washes down my face,
my back, my hands,
until I am clean.

November 13, 1998

An ordinary evening,
Friday, no less, in a
town seven hundred
miles from where you

live happily married.
sheets of rain seen
In the streetlights, not
quite translucent, color

life a darker shade.
A chill in the air,
winter in the South,
mirrors my mood

when I first stand on
the porch. Yet a cup of
coffee in my hand helps
warm me to my soul,

and what I like best is
the way the cup continues
to heat one's hands even
when the coffee is gone.

Molecular Biology

Every seven years,
like the locusts
or an itch, depending
on who you ask,

our bodies completely
regenerate, according
to scientists. Every
cell, replaced by

another, so that our
legs and ligaments,
arms and ankles, and
even our skull and

scapula are all new,
cellularly speaking.
While even our
membranes change,

though, our memories
somehow remain intact,
as well as memories
do, anyhow. So I

still remember your
legs and ligaments,
arms and ankles, and,
yes, your skull and

scapula, too. Though science tells
me they are new, they have not
changed in my mind or heart,
which are not the same at all.

Wedding Water

As you go to get me
more water,

not as Rebekah did for
Isaac's servant, moving her
toward marriage, and

not as the Samaritan woman
at the well did for Jesus as
an unknowing prelude to

theological thoughts and
the revealing of the men
she had married, but

simply because you think I
look thirsty, I ask you to
wait one moment

so that I might tell you
one true thing

so that you will
love me forever.

40 Days Won't Be Long Enough For Me

As soon as you
departed, I proceeded
to the park
as was our previous
practice--before you
left, that is.

And there I watched
the couples parade in
their paddle
boats, two by two, like

the lucky animals
into Noah's ark,
progressing into the
future safety of
coupledom and conception,

safe from the deluge of
singlehood, a death by drowning
in loneliness. And all the
while, I wait beside the
lake, grateful for the
coming rain.

Taking a Beating, Again

The boxes were packed and
stacked, waiting for moving

day, but before I could turn
toward the U-haul, love blind-

sided me like a local in a
barroom brawl. The befuddled

moving men could not
understand my battered and

bruised body, nor can they hear
the way my heart now pumps,

through the miracle of resurrection,
like the jukebox in the juke

joint where I lost that first
fight but won my first love.

Lover's Leap At Rock City

The trees far below
will either soften your
fall or break every

bone, as you bounce
from limb to limb on
your way down to the

ground. Love will do the
same, if only you have
the courage to hurl

yourself into her waiting
arms, stretched out like
the branches of a tree.

Narrative Delights

And while my poetry might
pine for the *sturm und drang*
of the past, the thunder and

lightning of betrayal and
jealousy that fueled
fictions and propelled

plots to their denouement of
resolution and writing, my
tastes in stories have

deepened to include a
conclusion of apple pie
pressed against a cool

counterpoint of vanilla or the
introduction of a quilt in the
midst of winter, heating my

hands and heart for five
more minutes.

Maybe these are luxuries
in life, but so is this.
And so are you.

Free Fall

The story spills from
your lips like a
waterfall thawing after the
long winter of secrecy,

and the nervousness in
your eyes sets the
tone of the conversation like

the backscore of a
slasher film.

You close your eyes,
unable to endure the
emotional outburst of

shame and shock that is
sure to follow your confession,

but you still spreadeagle
yourself in the vacuum
of hope and love,

looking for a hand
to hold

but as you fall, worst
case scenarios flash
through your heart:

already feeling the tears,
knowing which CDs and
t-shirts need to be returned,

separating your books from
mine, and collecting your

shampoo and toothbrush
from my shower,

and then I catch you.

Et Tu?

Afterwards, you look for
the beginning, the big bang
that portended the end. But
the beginning is not found
in major implosions or explosions;

instead, it comes from small
details, minor events, and
injuries ignored who conspire
like courtiers planning a
coup, whispering behind your

back as you plan for a major
military offensive against the
current king of your concerns.
And as your minions map out
your battle plan, they slit your

throat while you sleep, not
even allowing you a final cry
for help or one more word of
wisdom, which you still believe
could have prevented this plot.

The Myth of You and Me

Introduced by a friend because of our love
for movies, we spent our early days in the
dark, watching lives of action and passion,
which we discussed over dinner, dissecting
cinematography and casting, plugging
plot holes while twirling fettuccini on
our forks, as tight as the end of a Hollywood
blockbuster. And so we created a home
theater system, with a television
large enough to hold new lives
every night and a system to surround
us with sound, blocking out the noise of
the world~wars and rumors of war~so
that we can eat together, our pasta, in peace.

Night Sky

Prophets of doom and
soothsayers see every
streak of lightning
as a crack in the
sky~World War III,

the second coming, or
some type of divine
judgment ("hell in
a handbasket" is only
a cliché if you don't

believe it's true).
But apocalypse
has never been my forte.
I prefer my eschatology
with a heaping spoonful

of hope~grace, rather
than judgment; some
deus ex machina will
surely save the world
we try to destroy, though

the question is moot:
my end times are now,
whether it be by a bomb
ticking in Tel Aviv or
the ceasing of the

ticking in my chest,
so I seek solace in
your arms until then,
and no *Maranatha*
will cross my lips,

God save my soul.

About the Author

Kevin Brown is an Associate Professor of English at Lee University. His poems have appeared in *The New York Quarterly*, *REAL: Regarding Arts and Letters*, *Connecticut Review*, *South Carolina Review*, *h2so4*, *Jeopardy*, and *The Pacific Review*, among other journals. He has also published essays in *The Chronicle of Higher Education*, *Academe*, *InsideHigherEd.com*, *The Teaching Professor*, and *Eclectica*. He is also the author of a book of scholarship, *They Love to Tell the Stories: Five Contemporary Novelists Take on the Gospels*.

LaVergne, TN USA
21 September 2009
158491LV00001B/3/P

9 781935 514343